How to Enter the River
Poems by Jeanie Thompson

How to Enter the River

Poems by Jeanie Thompson

Introduction by Pamela Stewart

Holy Cow! Press · IOWA CITY, IOWA · 1985

ISBN 0-930100-18-2

Library of Congress Number: 84-062337

Photograph of Jeanie Thompson by Frank Morgan

Cover photograph © 1985 by Wayne Sides

First Printing

I am grateful to the Louisiana State Arts Council through the Division of the Arts for a generous Artistic Fellowship which allowed me time to write and revise portions of this book.

Printed in the United States of America.

Publisher's Address:
Holy Cow! Press
Post Office Box 2692
Iowa City, Iowa 52244

This project is supported by a grant from the National Endowment for the Arts in Washington, D.C., a Federal agency.

for Richard

TABLE OF CONTENTS

V.

INTRODUCTION

We live today in a fearsome world, one in which we dare not always trust to a happy future, if any future at all. And yet, scientifically and spiritually, we have never known the world and its place within the universe so intimately. We have never been so informed of, nor perplexed by, its range of mysteries. That's both exciting and frightening, and there has never been so much to write about, for even the-same-old-things are transformed by context. Of course we continue to look to the past to align the place of where we are in hopes of some irrefutable clue to the future. But, as many do, to *only* lament the loss of the past, of anything, is one-dimensional and enforces a repetitive poetry of demi-jeremiads.

To turn a grave yet affectionate heart towards the face of this world as it is, while simultaneously regarding one's past, requires a fairmindedness that is both difficult and, at times, heartrending to sustain. *How to Enter the River* does just that, for it is a rare sort of book, a declaration of faith. While the poet's past receives both tough appraisal and a wistful scrutiny, Jeanie Thompson's vision and assessment retain a gentle and generous dignity. Memory is never weakened nor wrenched into deluded, sentimental imagery. One indication of Thompson's spiritual will is when the voice of a girl-child speaks. Such a voice is consistently filtered and made live through that of a grown woman. As Thompson's poetic intention evolves, the child and the woman take on one flesh—an embrace—even as the child is absent. This is the case when the poet speaks of her own past and its connection to the present, as well as when she imagines the beloved child she would wish to have had herself. Despite the loss, Thompson's ability to love continues, treated with a strength of character. *How to Enter the River* shows how the insistence of love where "there is nothing / more real than this place" may withstand the intrusive cruelties delivered by the indifference of the world. Thompson's poems are never reduced to bitterness. Understanding and experiencing loss itself begins to fill in the absence. As she tells us in the graceful sequence "The Songs Beyond Hearing," it is for the everlasting sake of the *living* that she herself has chosen to live, that her poems live. Even those few poems where Thompson speaks as, or for, a character removed by history or literature, her clear-seeing, effective conveyence of emotion brings the character alive, yearning. Behind the poet's need to speak directly and inevitably, the scaffolding of artifice is barely noticeable. Caught up by their appropriateness, one reads these poems without being uncomfortably conscious of manner or strategy. Thompson's work reminds the diligent reader that pain, joy, desire, loss—the articulation of life for life's sake—may always draw strength from generosity, hope and moral will. The current of bravery threading this book, along with the single-minded commitment to love, show how Jeanie Thompson's poetry deserves our grateful attention for its fine clarity, resilience, and determination that we, and the larger world, shall not fail. Must not.

Pamela Stewart
St. Ives, Cornwall 1984

I.

In The Darkened Ballroom

I've entered late
giddy with anticipation,
and hear
the hard words of my schoolmates
soften like cotton in the mouths
of young men and women
reunited in a darkened ballroom.
When an innocent-faced wife says, *Jeanie,*
I remember how her hits in softball
astounded everyone,
her thin ankle grinding the dust
and the sure *thunk* as the ball
met the blond bat.
Awkward in our red gymsuits
we had toyed with sports,
conspired for the boys
now grown languid and pot-bellied.
Before I can speak
or introduce my husband
I'm standing for photographs
with the same mute group
as years before.
The ones I loved
for our childhood hours
return, happy to see me.
I have returned safe, too.
And the girl I loved for her beauty
is coming through the door
and still has the same golden head—
her smile reaches me
as something I might touch.
Whatever terrible secrets
we have all kept from one another
vanish in the protective dark
where we embrace
and dance, touching
as if for the first time.

On My 29th Birthday I Remember

My train has stopped
in the grey station
of my birthplace:
I see a man
trudge across the gravel
from working 30 years
for the Southern Railroad.
I would like to meet him
but what will I say?
That I know
we are born of simple flesh?
That the tiny precise atoms
of our bodies
are the same atoms
swirling in fiery galaxies
a hundred light years away?

I look past the station
to the red clay hills
choked with kudzu:
I know there is nothing
more real than this place.
I feel my heart rise
without reason of name or place
and touch the land.
Here at this lonely depot
the only person
on the platform is a woman.
If I could speak to her,
I think, if only
I had the courage to say,
Love continues
like light falling upon earth.
This is heartland—

anywhere we step,
when the light
suddenly shatters
in a thousand filaments of belief.

For My Father

The child you hold
sits wide awake,
rapt, for *Scuppers the Sailor Dog.*
For you the words form
regularly into patterns
bound between the covers
of this Little Golden Book.
But for her, there are no words,
though sounds paint the sailor dog
asleep in his cabin, on his ship,
sailing his own sea.

I want to sit on the bed's edge
and listen.
You see, but motion me away.
Still, I raise the spy-glass
and the world's soft features
align themselves.

I wish we could reach back
across the water,
the pine-green sea of the story,
and touch
like two heads bowed above a book.
I wish I could pull on the garment
of Scuppers' character
as she wore it, for warmth,
for imagined safety,
as she entered his world
and her own, forming one word,
crossing the water into sleep.

OCTOBER: THE FACT OF TREES

I.

In Alabama, memory peels the yellowed
photograph of your father.
He is still young, handsome in his bowler hat.
All his brothers are smiling as if he's
the one who'd told the joke. The fact of him
will not change, though we leave the cemetery
where one red tree flames out of itself.

You want to drive further north,
to see the red and gold and purple,
those leaves that blush now
a new, unfamiliar color.
The wind will carry them off
and you find yourself chasing them.

You might dig the clay for the colors
but the grit, worked under your fingernails,
comes alive in your skin at night.
In dreams you tear at gloves of pain
grown like bark to your hands,
impossible as memory to be stripped clean.

II.

This year a foreign autumn kisses
and steals the trees. It is Indian summer.
The birches that border the yard flame gold,
then drop their leaves overnight.
You would throw them back to the trees
but the colors burn your fingers.

Firs and pines hold armfuls of snow
as an offering. Even these do not satisfy,
standing green and blue all winter. You know

their needles are sharp, sticky with resin,
though they hold this heavy blanket of snow up to you:
A gesture like wind layering snow
in New England, rain in Alabama.

I see faces in the leaves
the way children see things at night.
I know the leaves are leaves,
as the child does, but see the faces still.
When I think of you
it is at that point
between the leaf and the face,
between memory
and the fact that you are not here.

for my mother

Dear Louie,

Tonight I couldn't work and started dreaming
over the photo on my desk—
the one I took of you
and Stephanie that New Year's Eve.
Waiting for the streetcar, you both
face into the New Orleans mist,
the streetlights two red moons.
She leans against you
comfortably: I was just learning
to know her then. You clutch
your tourist's package of who-knows-what
and hold her, a smile
about to break over your face.

This week I knew I should call you—
there is a grief we share.
I thought of one day
when you sat reading me
a poet we will both miss.
I was suspended on the moment, not knowing
if you knew. I thought of you
slugging through the mud
in the hospital parking lot,
the drunks and kids
just shaking themselves awake.

A friend shouldn't be afraid
giving news of pain—
but I was unable to see you
doing a job, loving your wife,
these things that
if I could know them daily,
would bring me comfort,
beyond words.

Obeying My Hands

What lets me forget you?
Nothing.
Tonight as I scrub the copper pot,
I know you'll never do this again.
How simple a thing to remember you by—
but you are in me as I circle
the sponge efficiently in soap,
will the pot to come clean.
These could be your hands.
Move, work, move, they tell me,
and I do it,
because I can make no sense
of your dying, or my hands,
little masters, urging me on.

for Kay Dorsch

WINTER PSALM

Your window opens
on the Florida night.
Gulls waken over the lake;
the hibiscus blooms
blood-orange.
Tangibles: the salt breeze,
the hibiscus flower,
a gull-cry.
This morning you'll send
your step-daughter to pick grapefruit.
This thought hardens in your mind:
Fifteen, watching me die.

In the shower,
rinsing away, rinsing away
the fever. Your face in the mirror
leaner, thinner.
Is it possible
a man could cease
to recognize himself?
The doctor promises months
but you think of moments—
the moment when the pain stops,
the moment when hunger returns.

A man is dying.
I try these words in my mouth.
At the airport, your eyes
broke through the medicine's lock
and you stared in hard pain
past all of us.
Your wife hugged me longer, tight.
I won't see you again.

*

I want to believe life
intensifies near the end.
Yesterday the sky
promised spring in January
and I walked, wanting spring
more than anything.
The clouds dimmed the city
and the chill came back.

*

Noon, the birds are singing
high in the pecan trees,
I feel such a longing to walk out
under them, I can't name
this desire which takes hold,
promising to carry me beyond pleasure
if I walk under birdsong
in a false spring.

*

Uncle, I imagine you sleep
and your wife dozes.
Perhaps death will come as softly
as the call no one hears
though a world diminishes,
though you believe in this moment
your voice reaches us.
At home I want to forget
the looks across a room that said,
Today I'm alive and happy to be living,
Today I'm with you and happy to be here.

But today you are dead, and 1000 miles away
I write these words in winter, to remember.

for Charles Wade

II.

To love the dead is easy.
They are final, perfect.
But to love a child
is sometimes to fail at love
while the dead look on
with their abstract sorrow.

—William Matthews

THE SONGS BEYOND HEARING

I. *Prelude*

Woman, come here.
I have a story and two pearls.

The story:
When I look in the mirror,
my face dissolves.
Who will stand in my place?

Two pearls:
One for each child
plucked out like valuables.

II. *Meditations for a Child*

You cannot imagine how long
I have wanted to speak to you.
I have been waiting to speak to you
a long, long time.
When I lean over you,
I smell what is you
rising from the soft
mystery just under your hair.

Your life
fully imagined
is not enough to make you
real. You woke
in someone else's life.
Your cry lifted into the night.

He and I were learning
to be each other's parents.
We wished we could behave

bravely enough
to be scolded by anyone.

But we left each other
in the absence of a dream,

we woke alone
to no sound,
a name we kept calling.

III. *This Silence*

A few of us gather
around a brown spill of earth.
There is a wooden box, so small
it couldn't possibly hold you.
Your father wants
to break his own hands.
The sky, an unendurable blue
like the print of my skirt
molding me in the dry wind.

Because I heard you calling,
because for brief moments
we touched,
I imagine that even lifting you
sleepless and breathless
is not more painful
than this absence, this silence.

IV. *There is nothing in your body that lies.*

Desire, or the memory of desire?

My hands move over his body.
They remember its ridges
and hollows. The fragile
cheekbones, vaguely Indian.
Still, his eyes go thin
and continuous when desire
rises in him. His hands
work me with patience
though my body stays sullen as dough.

I used to concentrate
that pull longing
for his seed
and I blossomed.

V. *Songs Beyond Hearing*

How easily I let you go!
When they came to cut
from me three stars,
your possible being,
I let go of your small hands,
closed each eye
with a thumbprint
rinsed the ink
from your shriveled heels.

I dreamed:
A woman enters a garden
and sits by a pond, trailing
her hand in the water.
With the keenest of knives
she cuts her own body,
offering her flesh to the water

where bloodless it dissolves.
She bathes her feet, arms and face.
Overhead the sky rinses blue.

Later, she sings as she gathers
fragrant branches of jasmine,
oleander from the garden's edge.

Beyond the boundary
of the garden
another woman gives up her life.
Shivering near her cold flesh,
a sleeping child grows restless, wakes.

VI. *In the Same World*

Awakened from a dream
of my life's end
knowledge grows in me:

What I have let pass from me
travels light years
beyond my claiming.

Now, I turn my face
from a world of darkness.
If I dream

it is not of the dead,
but of the living
for whose everlasting sake

I open my body's heart.

III.

Letters To The Isle Of Lesbos

I.

This shell of the hawksbill won't warm into song
for you or anyone, these strings

and our separation make things clearer,
clouding the past like the tortoise-shell's

milky reds, yellows, and browns.
Today I've walked for hours through cypresses

tossed by a late summer wind.
I long for the stillness of olive groves

heavy with fruit, a song for you,
I would sing just for you,

my fingers barely touching the strings.

Once I saw a girl gathering jonquils and anemone.
She chose blossoms for her hair

bright as torchlight.
It was then I closed my eyes

and the wind became a voice
carrying my song,

pressing against her,
molding the soft shapes of her tunic.

I imagined her translucent skin
growing warm at this touch.

when the sun fell,
like a coin dropped for luck into the Aegean,

I could believe in signs from heaven
as pure as the song rising from the warm sea

touching a young girl   who knows nothing.

II.

I dreamed your mouth was the lotus flower
opening in a kiss.
Your lips were pale petals
tinged with silver.
As I brush my hair loose,
the feel of it lifting off my shoulders
with the night wind
is like your hand, reaching to pull me back.
Tonight no one notices me walking alone
along the shore.
Rocks bruise my bare feet.
Night opens on the marble cliffs, spectres
flicker, indistinct as the dead,
gone when the creamy moon rises . . .

We lay on the bleached rock
and couldn't speak. My nightdress
dampening on the beach.
You loosened the purple band
from my loop of hair.
Against your warm skin
the moon was a light breath.
I believed for that moment
she was benevolent,
covering us with soft, yellow light.

But tonight, beside the black pool
of the sea, the moon seeps into my skin.
In a country as far away as death,
you walk toward me. Your arms, strong
as the limbs of an olive tree, lift me
to be kissed, but the moon's fragrant lips
touch my eyes in sleep.
As you lower me to the rocks
I take no notice
if they welcome me with small gifts,
jewels of purple and black. I am joining you

along Acheron, to watch the moist flower open.

Marie Laurencin's Portrait of Apollinaire

In your heart a scar is forming and grows with your silence.
The colors chosen for your portrait pale
against your friends. You look out from the diminishing
white field; the corners of your mouth droop.
One day you fear you will wake, the only scar left.

In another field a piece of shrapnel glows
in the skull of a man. What he sees is his body borne away
on a canvas stretcher. Watching me walk once you claimed
the wine trembled. I walked away. When I looked for you
at dusk among the foliage I caught your dark
suit, suddenly turning back. I think as you pour the wine

how the goblet seeks the translucent red line.
That for too long it has been this scene:
We are smoking in a café and your eyes are colorless
against the streets of this city. Rising above our heads
like the prayers of peasants, the wine catches
the evening and holds it, just briefly. A portrait, breaking open.

The Black Venus

If I dress for you in cheap, stage jewels
unwinding this coarse, black hair to my breasts,
I forget that the theatre was half-full tonight
of drunks and garish women,
the young men who always smell of wine or urine
standing outside the door,
throwing paper flowers at my feet.

You place a giant bowl of milk
at my feet and ask me to drink from it
like a cat with my pink tongue. You say
my hands are rough and beg me
to stroke your poor, tired head.
The lines you read while unbuttoning

your shirt mean nothing.
It is enough for the wine and what
I like better. Later, if you stay
I may allow you to curl on my breasts
tangling my hair for comfort, muttering curses
because you think you are near my heart.

If I close my eyes
there is a deep black forest
where a lover brings me fruit.
The sound of wind
through the broad-leaved trees is cool
and the perfume in my blood tells me
who I am and what I have always been.

Midnight Swim: For Marilyn Monroe

Night for you is the deep violet
rising from Victorian brownstones
in twilight Manhattan.
But here in Hollywood, each dive is pure gold
and the water shedding your skin, alive.
Where once every barroom wall
held a blonde nude on crimson velvet,
now you step from flesh-colored tights
to toss silver dollars at the screen.

Unable to sleep you float
in a pink diaphanous nightgown
through studio streets, returning
to the camera, still trusting
only its clear eye reversing you.
And facing the best of friends,
a hundred feet of silent color film,
you wink and dive
rising with a laugh.
Your platinum star spills into darkness
and is lost returning.

His Confession At Mid-Afternoon

All day I dug the creek bed for your colors.
I wanted to cover your face with a mask
of raw sienna. I wanted to cast
your laughter in rose madder.
But color couldn't hold the light of a star
as its spark took life in you

running up to me through the creek.
I offer white canvas to dry your legs
as you spread the wet skirt on the grass.
How long since
you sat simply for me by the window,
removed your purple felt hat, letting
your hair fall over one eye.
Where it touched your shoulder

I called it Indian yellow.
You were warm and slipped the satin
scarf from your long muscular throat.
My fingers later left a flush
I couldn't paint. I wanted only

the colorless wash of air and skin.
This morning
I took the camel-hair brushes
and rinsed each one in the creek,
stirring for a trace of blond or indigo

but your face would not appear.
Now as I lie here, still, inside you,
I don't need to say your hair
feels like thick wheat against my cheek,
or your skin smells like rain.

The Children

Smoke from her kitchen
rises to scent the bare tree
where a cardinal sings,
then dives for scattered bread.
On the lake below,
Allison tightens her skates
and begins her figures.
She moves through the winter air
tensing muscle and bone
to steel, to ice
and enters the pure motion
of her body.

Chloe is tired but doesn't sleep:
His finger traced the arc of her nose
and down across her cheek —
she can't believe it happened!
She turns and pulls the quilt
close to her mouth. His hard muscles
shocked her
like her face in the mirror,
flushed and bright.

When she wakes, her sister's bed empty,
she hesitates, remembering
the dream of a forest,
a touch, and the unfamiliar
breath of someone beside her.

*

Her children at play
or still sleeping,
she sits alone
and watches the cardinal,

its orange beak a small fire
among brown feathers.

She thinks of Chloe
already dreaming the day
she will leave this house.
Now the cardinal bobs on a branch,
almost hurled, almost in flight
against the winter sky.

Everything she is
will rise away from her
impossible to keep.

IV.

BIRCH STREET: 1960

A woman was always singing in that house
and we played a game called "Mother"
at the Pughs' across the street.
I was oldest, had to be "it." My duties were:
scold Barbara, caress Bev and Amy, keep
house, keep peace, like a real mother.
We drew the world's boundaries—
kitchen, child's room, door.

A woman was always singing—
the real house, not the make-believe one
where I was too unsure to carry a tune.
A woman's voice
singing cool songs with confidence
was always there. Sometimes it came
from the kitchen, sometimes, the phonograph.
I couldn't tell the difference,
so when I heard the voice,
I believed it was you,
your cigarette burning in the ashtray
while you buttered bread,
sliced roast beef for our sandwiches,
poured milk—small green mugs
for us, little girls playing house.

Today I put on Ella Fitzgerald singing Cole Porter,
sat in the rocker and listened. I wanted
to hear *you*. I thought
I might smell Bev's clean, powdery smell,
my "daughter" who has her own baby now,
who doesn't remember, she's told me,
living in the house,
no childhood more special
than any other.

When I read favorite books sometimes
I find my comments in the margins,
"important," a lone initial "T," or
a passage in brackets that once explained
me to myself. Reading today,
I erased what I found, wanting the book clean.

for Eugenia Pugh

AT THE WHEELER WILDLIFE REFUGE

I. The Observation Building

The little girl in line for the telescope
says, "Look! Them birds are black pepper!"
and turns, grinning, surprised at herself.
Beyond the wall of glass, the flock
rises to light across the bare river bank.

"That bird's crazy," someone whispers.
But the sparrow hawk is dancing in place
50 yards up, wings beating
as if its power draws nothing from the earth.
For a second its wings flash
open, stilled, then it dances again
and falls from sight.

II. Walking the Trail

Winter wheat, rabbit tobacco, sorghum
dried to a dark rattle.
Harvest of sparse color in a dry wind.
And thorns low on the ground,
a network of warning.
Beyond this miniature trail, cornfields
spread green in winter grass.
I stop walking to face the far-off, solid
stand of pines. I tilt my head back:
the air is sweet. Closing my eyes,
I breathe again,
there's no other word,
so I lay my head back, breathing
as deep as a blue-tick hound
when the scent floods past
rank and scared for life.

When I leave this place
I'll take the fourlane
cutting through the backwater.
What tells me I'm alive
is impossible, useless to carry away.

How To Enter The River

Now the singing of the river is his.
He has opened his eyes and each tree
in its green integrity
bows as he moves past.
Beneath him, around him
the water is a muscle,
a heart of jewels spilled over rock.
He's forgotten his hand on the paddle,
his arm, continuous, dips
and pulls, guides the boat
to enter the river, unnoticed.

He keeps his back turned
as his children pry effortlessly
through the rapids,
sure of their skill, that they feel
where the boat must go. Still,
there is a sadness
in his straight, impassive back,
as if by turning from them,
he insures they will go on
paddling forever, forever his,
here among lighted waters,
flexing, opening around him
in song.

for Mickey Landry

Desire

The dream repeats its motif:
I reach toward you but you move
through my gesture
even as you turn your face away.
A young woman skirts the edge;
she only complicates
what we cannot change.

What does it mean to have lost you,
One I never had?

Last time we were together
I sat talking with you,
managing the conversation
like a tangible burden we share.
Once in a silence, I wanted to smooth
my hands over your whole body
to make sure you were there, become
what I knew you to be.

I watched desire, as if it can exist apart,
like a squall approaching over water.
At the edge of the thunderclouds
I saw rain, imagined
mist dampening my arms
as the wind picked up.
Suddenly I was on the other side.
I turned and saw behind me
the blue-grey filaments moving away
as the storm delivered to the land
its sheer, ardent body.

ALLEGRO ASSAII

In the darkness of the car
Bach's double concerto caught us
though we sped over the black plane
of an Arkansas night, heading north.
Ahead, heat lightning,
clouds gathering in on themselves.
Your hand
rested, a still bird on your knee.
The storm pulsed *adagio*
as if in time to the bass,
the soaring, plaintive violinfire.

That night I tried to tell you
how the violins in the *allegro assaii*
spoke, one to another, of passion and reason.
What I didn't say
was that the music was like the release
in the dancer's arc, past time:
an utterance perfected before my hearing.
Driving blindly toward music I desired,
I followed as if God had given us
this storm for a beacon.
Still, I wonder what you heard,
what charge imprinted your heart that night.
Did light and music dance
in such a way for you
that you believed we understood
anything was possible?

THE PAST WE SEE

It's the past we see in the sky:
Light traveling to our eyes before sight,
before the cell blinked its division
or matter journeyed into itself.

Like a star caught clear in the autumn sky
I saw a child looking toward me, her face
turned upward, her eyes hurtling past mine.
Memory's precision is no better

than the fat jay digging under a wing
as he sits in the pecan tree.
His sharp warning silenced, he returns
to the elements of motion and fire.

Look away, he's gone. Forget her eyes, and space
closes—stars calling we've never answered.

HAPPINESS

What is happiness but a way to see things?
Last night after my run, I bathed, lingering
over my preparations, then, into the bedroom
where you were watching baseball on TV.
I lay down nude on the bed, opened my book.
Once you turned to me after Reid Nichols
made a fantastic play for the Red Sox and grinning
you said, "That was marvelous, did you see it?"
I hadn't, but on the replay I watched him feel
for the wall, his glove ready,
then rocket the ball to second for the double play.
It washed over me that we were happy,
in this moment, though we didn't touch,
though what pleased us was simple.
How could we be happier?

Seasonal

I.

First day of school
I pack my new book satchel,
smelling its secrets of plaid cotton
and leather buckles.
Here is the red and gold pencil
so thick I can barely use it.
Here is the brown paper sack
and the orange's juicy spores
releasing forever into the autumn morning.

II.

In the room you've drawn the curtain
against the light. Stirring,
you say my name in a drowsy voice
that comes from far away.
Intruder, ready to be saved,
I crawl into the warm bed,
the smell of sleep holds me gently
as if it were somehow wrong, Mother,
to be here in my new dress,
wanting you.

RETURNING

In my old neighborhood again it's cold, November
and the reds and golds of maple, ginko I collect

are far too vivid for memory. I walk, holding a handful
of leaves speckled with rot. I turn the familiar

corner past the Lacys' house, and I'm twelve years old.
The sound of wind through white pine and sweet gum

soothes, as necessary as a lullaby. When a cat at ten yards
emits a sound like speech, I stop to answer her.

The wind nudges, mouthing a script in the leaves
scattering like children across the high green lawns.

Now at the school yard, drawn by the screech and cheers
of recess, the teacher stands, poker stiff in the wind,

watching a game of kickball. Her blue skirt and brown sweater,
her dark glasses firm against the winter sun.

The tall pines brush each other like shy girls.
The woman stands, still watching me

racing against the ball, my foot cocked—
I turn the corner, allowing memory and childhood

their moment near one another, so quiet,
these patient neighbors.

Snowy Egrets Flying Before A Storm

Thunderclouds gathered above the highway
like a bruise rising to the surface of the sky.
I crossed the Mississippi and rain fell,
the world became water, grey matter.

In the stillness just ahead of the storm
I saw snowy egrets lifting above a field.
Their bodies rose, a chorus
catching the currents of the mightier air.
Their flock twisted and whipped,
a delicate net of feather, wing and bone
that broke as the storm flew into them
and I felt the fear hold me
and I flew with it.

AFTER A WINTER

We drove through the Blue Ridge,
our first visit after a long separation,
your body healing at last.
Broom sedge shifted like winter wheat
among the grey trees.
We climbed higher, and saw below us
the mountains like a herd of camels
who'd strayed into Virginia.
Kneeling, their long necks tucked down,
they slept in the foreign earth.
Anita, how did I know you were forgiving
a child lost to you?

Later, in the bare maples
four young does
grazed close to the highway.
When I asked you stopped the car.
Each dipped her head in turn
and blinked fathomless eyes.
I rolled down the window
to make a noise in my throat,
as close as I could come to praying.
Catching the human scent
one stepped near us,
raised an athletic neck,
signaled her white tail
as if a calf were near.
The cold suspended us
and I heard every stillness
in her body cry *live*.

THINKING OF KAY IN GRASMERE

On an afternoon like this
  you taught me afternoon tea
    but I never knew why you poured milk
over the back of a spoon into your cup.
  Something British, a habit I witnessed,
    but never understood.

Kay, it's spring here, green everywhere.
  The fig tree abloom in her gauzy leaves
    as if life were all green infusion.
I am afraid of not saying what I mean:
  You are dying;
    I won't see you again.

After school, I boil water, warm the pot,
  exhausted, thinking how today I saw words
    skip and dodge just out of my grasp.
Children's faces, skin taut and clear.
  Tentative, one handed me a poem,
    pressed his small body against mine.

Remember our talks about children?
  The children I'll never know,
    your daughter's you'll never see.
Who are these people? Thoughts we conjure?
  I want to ask hard if they're real,
    or have any meaning, because today I know

you near that place where all
  unborn children are. I could
    imagine mine, blond and fair,
or dark in their secret habits, but what
  use is that? I've done with them, living apart,
    lost in their own world.

Last night I dreamed of England,
   the country where I'd hoped to see you
     delighting in the bright cardinals you love.
Today, my hands gesture as if to touch your face—
   I would pour strong tea in a china cup,
     I would define the exact angle of yellow-

skirted daffodils in sunlight. Pitilessly, the world
  shines on into spring, in New Orleans, where
     one living child dreams the image for *sunrise*.
He picks his words eagerly, breathing them
   in and out, the simple choice
     all that is necessary, friend, for speech.

V.

TINDER DREAMING OF SMOKE

prelude: Woodcut With Lovers

Tonight water wraps
its warm tentacle around us
Firecolors: orange, red, yellow
glisten like our
underwater shadow
A star illumines your chest
and weeping limbs

I stream into you,
through your body,
that sieve of flame
Water fills the world around us,
a reminder
it began this dance

Your Arrival

Morning sighed her breath of fog
long, langorous

Red globes of streetlights
hung like bright apples on a bow

Reaching, my hand led me
through the grey wall of fog

You arrived this way

I entered and entered you,
beloved, receding just beyond me

I said *Yes* opening my arms
and breathed you in,
clear air,
morning flooded with light

Love-making After a Silence

Not of words, but of our bodies
near each other, like tinder

dreaming of smoke
When you touched me

I saw the road open like a purple flower
I remember that I saw this!

I stayed in place,
but the touching led me

I saw the whiteness
as a bird with outstretched wings

He hovered toward me, above me,
my body winnowing like fire at his touch

Out of the silence he came to me
I had no name to call him

I see the wings still—
and long for him

Pleasure, After the Mind's Work

Pleasure, after the mind's work,
recklessly spent us—

I said to my arms
be the bird's wing
as I hovered over you

We were sailing into an open sea
we were racing—

Our storm
like a net cast
over a sleeping body

Tangled within each other
we drifted
I heard your breath, deep below me

Your hand
covered my fingers
the shape of gulls skimming water

Song of the Black Iris

Black iris! Unpeel your light—
you are like Man and Woman,
a world of opposites

Your petals gather like fog
on a mountain top,
your petals reveal
a tunnel of fathomless dark

Winging open like the lips
of a woman just giving birth,
your petals engorge with their secret

Wisest of flowers,
black iris,
you sheathe your rival—
At your center
the rosebud wakens,
plum-colored,

she says *Look at me*
I am fantastic
I will open
on your tongue

I am the beginning
of your life

Song, and a Charm Against the Marketplace

I enter the world, dressed by you
I whirl the skirt of your eyes,
taking in everything

In my hair, a gardenia,
ivory moonflower, its fragrance
trails just behind my ear
If I turn my head
you are that close

Around my neck
a string of miniature fruit—
For my ankles, bells of hammered silver

If you saw her,
would you recognize this festive woman?

Watch for her! When you hear silver
brushing against flesh
she may be dancing
free of the heavy coin in your hand

Song for My Body's Dancing

In my mother's womb, I danced
to the pulse
of our mingled bloods

My heart grew like a red drum
My fingers uncurled like Spanish fans
My feet opened and met,
curious waves

In my mother's womb I danced

My mother said, I stretched
my full length, fist to toe
dancing that stretch for the sun

No one said that a child
couldn't fly
No one said that my feet
couldn't move like a bird

As a girl I moved for joy—
for the reaching around the earth
A woman, I danced with men,
their arms like strong winds
lifting me out of myself

I learned my body's dancing
I chose to love, I chose you
With you I stretch,
meeting the earth, riding the wave

In the womb of our love, I dance!

Wed

When you go,
nothing will be real
I will have no one to tell

My body remembers in its smallchild bones
a schoolyard,
the taunt of smirking girls
I run, wanting to lose myself
in anything—
The earth opens like a pit,
the horizon takes a giant step away

Now your hand reaches me
or your face is there
in place of a final emptiness
As for our bodies,
they don't need our consent
Seeking each other for comfort,
they meet where thought breaks
and we slip free

In the dark,
night snuffs out each word
we might speak,
one hand over another
like a shell cradling a web of bone,
our dreams mingle deeper than blood

Oh my love,
may this telling keep the world
for us both!

NOTES

1. The title of Section IV of "The Songs Beyond Hearing" is a line from Anne Sexton's poem "Little Girl, My String Bean, My Lovely Woman."
2. "Letters to the Isle of Lesbos" makes use of some images from the fragments of Sappho's poems.
3. "Marie Laurencin's Portrait of Apollinaire" is based loosely on the relationship of the French poet and his lover. Several images in this poem are inspired by various translations of the ghazals of the Urdu poet Galib.
4. The first line of "The Past We See" is taken from Timothy Ferris's *Galaxies*.

Grateful acknowledgment is made to the editors of the following magazines in which some of these poems first appeared or are forthcoming:

Antaeus: "Marie Laurencin's Portrait of Apollinaire"
The Back Door: "Midnight Swim: For Marilyn Monroe"
The Black Warrior Review: "The Children"
Crazy Horse: "In the Darkened Ballroom" and "Thinking of Kay in Grasmere"
The Greensboro Review: "October: The Fact of Trees"
The Missouri Review: "Birch Street: 1960" and "At the Wheeler Wildlife Refuge"
New England Review: "The Songs Beyond Hearing"
New Virginia Review: "For My Father"
North American Review: "Returning"
Ploughshares: "Snowy Egrets Flying Before a Storm"
Pontchartrain Review: "Dear Louie"
Porch: "Letters to the Isle of Lesbos" as "To Lesbos"
raccoon: "His Confession at Mid-Afternoon"
Southern Humanities Review: "The Black Venus"
Telescope: "Obeying My Hands" and "Allegro Assaii"
Woman Poet: The South: "How to Enter the River"
Xavier Review: "On My 29th Birthday I Remember"

Several of the poems collected here appeared in *Lotus and Psalm*, a limited edition chapbook published by Baltic Avenue Press, Birmingham, Alabama.

Jeanie Thompson, a native of Alabama, attended The University of Alabama, where she edited *The Black Warrior Review* for its first four issues and received an MFA in Creative Writing. Her poems, interviews with poets, book reviews, and criticism have appeared in *Antaeus, Missouri Review, North American Review, Ironwood, Southern Quarterly* and others. She has taught at the University of New Orleans and in the Poets-in-the-Schools program in the Metropolitan New Orleans area. In 1980 Jeanie Thompson was the first recipient of the Louisiana State Arts Council Artist Fellowship in Literature. She lives with her husband, Richard Weaver, in Tuscaloosa, Alabama.